EDGE
BOOKS

⊹ INTO THE GREAT OUTDOORS ⊹

FRESHWATER
FISHING
For Kids

BY MELANIE A. HOWARD

Consultant:
Craig Bihrle
North Dakota Game and Fish Department
Bismarck, North Dakota

CAPSTONE PRESS
a capstone imprint

Edge Books are published by Capstone Press,
1710 Roe Crest Drive, North Mankato, Minnesota 56003.
www.capstonepub.com

Library of Congress Cataloging-in-Publication Data
Howard, Melanie A.
  Freshwater fishing for kids / by Melanie A. Howard.
    p. cm. — (Edge books: into the great outdoors)
  Includes bibliographical references and index.
  ISBN 978-1-4296-8422-4 (library binding)
  ISBN 978-1-4296-9269-4 (paperback)
  ISBN 978-1-62065-227-5 (ebook pdf)
  1. Fishing—Juvenile literature. 2. Freshwater fishes—Juvenile literature.
  I. Title.
  SH445.H69 2013
  597.176—dc23   2012006922

Editorial Credits

Brenda Haugen, editor; Ted Williams, designer; Marcie Spence,
    media researcher; Sarah Schuette, photo stylist; Marcy Morin,
    scheduler; Laura Manthe, production specialist

Photo Credits

Alamy: Gunter Marx, 29, Jana Thompson, 8-9, Karel Lorier, 28;
Bridgeman Art Library: Jamahirya Museum, Tripoli, Lybia, 8; Capstone
Studio: Karon Dubke, 15, 16; iStockphoto: princessdlaf, 23; Shutterstock:
ARENA Creative, 14, Dewitt, cover, 6 (inset), Fedor Kondratenko, 17, Julie
Keen, 20, Kevin H Knuth, 6 (back), Kevin R. Williams, 19, Kletr, 4-5, Mat
Hayward, 24, Matt Jeppson, 3, Mikael Damkier, 10-11, Rade Kovac, 1,
Steve Brigman, 26-27, Yevgen Timoshov, 12

Printed in the United States of America in Stevens Point, Wisconsin.
032012   006678WZF12

TABLE OF CONTENTS

CHAPTER 1

THE GREEN-EYED MONSTER

Your fishing pole tip dips. It's barely a tug. Maybe it's the bait bouncing off the bottom of the lake. But reeling in your fishing line, you spot a tiny walleye skimming the surface of the water. The fish is barely bigger than your bait.

The walleye is halfway to the boat when you see a V shape slice into the water. Suddenly the little walleye is dragged beneath the waves. You almost lose your grip on the pole as the line runs out with a high whirring sound. A great weight yanks against you. You brace the butt of the rod against your life vest. Your fishing pole nearly bends in half.

You reel in, fighting the rod tip out of the water. Grandpa grabs the net. A large northern pike glares up at you from just beneath the surface. Then the fish dives under the boat. With a great heave, you haul the pike back to the surface.

FACT
In 2008 North Carolina's channel catfish record was broken by a man and his granddaughter fishing with a toy Barbie Doll rod and reel. The fish was 2 inches (5 centimeters) longer than the rod.

pumpkinseed
sunfish

largemouth
bass on a jig

Grandpa scoops the net into the water and flips the northern pike into the boat. The pike isn't hooked at all. Its teeth are clamped onto the walleye!

Grandpa grins at you, and you grin back. "Look at that green-eyed monster," he says, clapping you on the back.

The pike is longer than your arm. It's a keeper.

STARTING WITH SUNFISH

Anglers new to the sport often start by fishing for sunfish. Sunfish come in many varieties, such as pumpkinseed and green. Bluegill, crappie, and black bass also belong to the sunfish family. Most sunfish reach a size of less than 8 inches (20 cm) long, but a black bass can be as long as 32 inches (81 cm) and weigh up to 22 pounds (10 kg).

Sunfish can be caught on simple weighted **baits** called jigs. They can also be caught on **spinnerbaits**, but often an angler will catch one using a float. This technique is also known as "bobber fishing." When bobber fishing, the angler keeps an eye on the float, or bobber. The bobber dangles a baited hook at a set depth in the water. If a fish hits the bait, the bobber will be pulled underwater. The angler sets the hook when the float plunges under the water.

Casting a bobber in a shallow area where there are weeds or sunken logs is a good way to catch sunfish. Sunfish are usually found in water that is no deeper than 30 feet (9 meters).

bait—something used to attract fish

spinnerbait—a fake bait with blades that spin when it is pulled through the water

All on the Line

People have been fishing for thousands of years. It was an important source of food. The first fishers used hooks made of bone, wood, or stone. They tied the hooks to vines and pulled them by hand. The Ancient Egyptians fished. So did the Greeks and Romans. The Chinese fished with bamboo rods and silk line as early as the 400s BC.

Fishing for sport started in the 1400s. People who fish for sport are fishing for fun and not just food. Since it began sport fishing has grown more popular. It's become a tradition in many families. It also has inspired many TV shows and led to an explosion of modern fishing equipment. Many competitions and records have sprung up around sport fishing.

Freshwater fishing is fishing for food or sport in bodies of water such as rivers and lakes. It is very popular in the United States. In fact, freshwater fishing has a Hall of Fame in Hayward, Wisconsin. The Fresh Water Fishing Hall of Fame and Museum displays equipment used for freshwater fishing over the years. It also keeps records of famous anglers and the largest freshwater fish caught around the world.

FACT
More than 50,000 people visit the Fresh Water Fishing Hall of Fame and Museum in Hayward, Wisconsin, every year.

CHAPTER 2

HOOK, LINE, AND SINKER

spinning reel
and rod

Modern fishing has come a long way from stone hooks and vines. Today's freshwater anglers use a variety of fake baits and equipment, such as **sonar** fish finders. A fish finder usually tells an angler the water depth. It also shows fish swimming in the water.

Freshwater anglers try to catch many kinds of fish. Many people enjoy fishing for largemouth bass because these fish are easy to catch.

Reel 'Em In

Most freshwater fishing is done with rods that go with baitcasting, spincasting, and spinning reels. Rods used with baitcasting reels are very stiff. They allow an angler to cast heavy bait more easily. A rod used with a spincasting reel is similar, but it is meant for a lighter bait and line. A rod used with a spinning reel is different. This rod's reel is mounted underneath the rod instead of on top. It is less ideal for casting, but it is more sensitive to a fish strike.

sonar—a device that uses sound waves to find underwater objects; sonar stands for sound navigation and ranging

A rod and reel should be chosen based on the kind of fishing you're going to do. For example, if you're fishing for walleye with a jig, you should use a spinning rod and reel. Then you can feel when the fish bites. Experience also matters. It's much easier for an angler with little experience to cast using a spincasting reel than a baitcasting reel.

Going after large or tough fish requires more strength, patience, and skill. The equipment needed also is more varied. The white sturgeon is the largest freshwater fish in North America. It can grow as big as 1,500 pounds (680 kg). To catch it, an angler may need a heavy-duty sea fishing rod and reel. Large catfish can also require a sea fishing rig.

CASTING

Unless you drop your bait straight over the side of the dock or boat, an angler must know how to cast. A cast is usually done overhead. But other types of casts include the horizontal, underhand, and flip.

A good cast needs two things: accuracy and distance. The best way to learn both is to practice. You can practice casting before you even go out on the water. Set targets such as hula hoops out in your yard. Fit your line with a casting weight instead of a hooked lure. See if you can cast the weight into the middle of the target. You should try to cast at least 25 feet (7.6 m). With practice, you'll likely be able to cast 50 feet (15 m) or more.

Getting a feel for when to release the line and still hit your target is something every angler needs to learn. To cast accurately, keep your eyes on the target. You're less likely to cast to the left or right of the target if you keep looking at it.

If you're casting a bait that sinks rather than floats, reel in faster when the bait hits the water to avoid snagging it on weeds. Then slow down after about 6 feet (1.8 m). The farther the bait gets from shore, the deeper the water usually is. When you slow down as you are reeling in, the bait begins to sink. This catches the attention of fish swimming in deeper water.

lure—a fake bait used in fishing

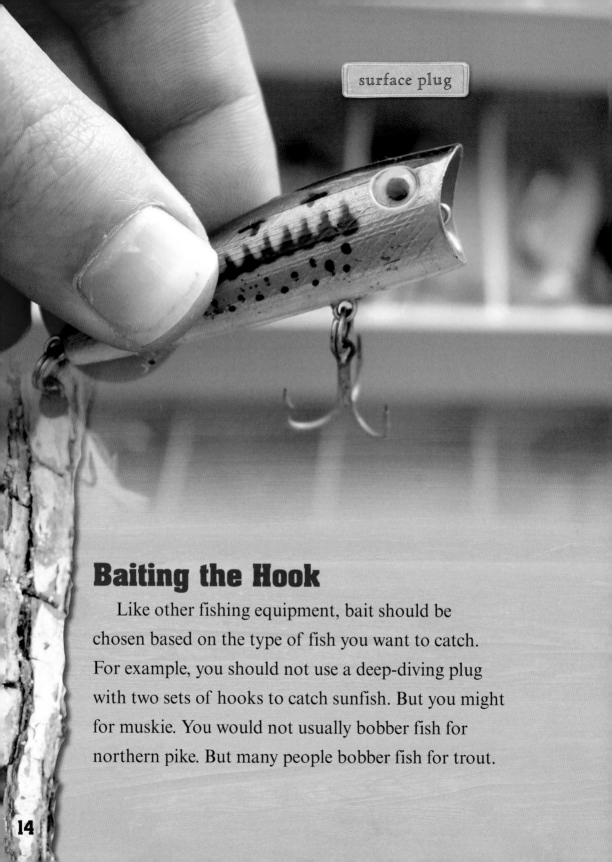

surface plug

Baiting the Hook

Like other fishing equipment, bait should be chosen based on the type of fish you want to catch. For example, you should not use a deep-diving plug with two sets of hooks to catch sunfish. But you might for muskie. You would not usually bobber fish for northern pike. But many people bobber fish for trout.

When it comes to fake and natural baits, the choices seem endless. Corn, crickets, shrimp, salamanders, eggs, frogs, and even squid can be used as bait. Baits that work for several kinds of fish include leeches, worms, and minnows.

Anglers use many different kinds of fake baits, depending on what they hope to catch. Spinners, soft plastic lures, and diving, sinking, and surface plugs fill many anglers' tackle boxes. Baits such as jigs are often paired with natural baits, such as worms, to catch fish.

waxworms

Sharp, Tough, and Ready to Go

No matter what you are fishing for, your gear takes a beating. It's important to check and maintain your equipment.

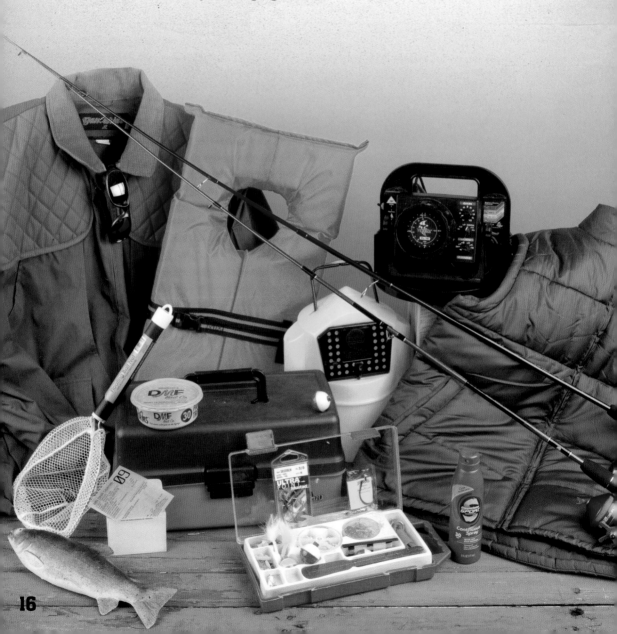

leader

Run your fingers over the last few feet of your line. It should feel smooth. If you detect a lot of roughness, follow your line until you reach a point where it feels smooth. Cut the bad line off. Chewed up line will snap easily. You don't want a northern pike to swim off with your favorite lure because you were fishing with bad line. And if you're angling for a fish that can cut line with its teeth, it's a good idea to protect your line and your bait by using a **leader**.

leader—a short piece of wire that connects a fishing line to the bait

Hooks will bend as you use them. You can bend a hook back into place with a pair of pliers. A bent hook won't hook a fish as well as a straight hook. You don't want your fish to slip off during a fight. Hooks also get dull over time and need to be sharpened.

Nets, **stringers**, and pliers are just a handful of the items in your tackle box to keep an eye on. They are used often and tend to wear out.

stringer—a string, wire, or chain with snaps that hold fish

FACT
Rods can also take a beating and may need attention. Grips may need to be rewrapped, and guides may need replacing. Missing guides may cause the line to rub against your rod. Always replace broken guides so your rod performs well.

CHAPTER 3

FISHING SAFETY

Making sure your equipment is well cared for and working properly also helps keep you safe. Safety is a big concern for anglers.

Safety Equipment

Most anglers spend some time fishing from a boat. Anytime you are in a boat, it's important to wear a life jacket. Sometimes it's the law. Choose a life jacket that fits you well, and wear it every time you are out on the water. Replace it when it wears out or if you outgrow it. A life jacket could save your life.

Hats, lightweight long-sleeved clothing, sunglasses, and boots are safety equipment too. Anglers spend a lot of time in the sun. They also spend time around biting bugs. You want to guard against sunburn and bug bites. Boots or even a sturdy pair of tennis shoes will protect your feet from rocky shorelines and misplaced sharp objects, such as hooks.

Hooks and Hands

Getting hooked is pretty painful. Hooks are sharp and usually have a **barb**. When fishing near other people, be very careful when casting. Double check to be sure people aren't going to get hit as you cast. Also try not to yank your lure out of the water when reeling it in. It could spring up and hit someone.

Anglers need to protect their hands from some types of fish too. Fish often have sharp back fins and teeth. Most anglers handle fish bare-handed, but fish gloves will help protect your hands. Gloves also help you get a better grip on slippery fish so you can unhook them more quickly.

barb—a sharp piece of metal that extends from behind a fish hook's point

Most anglers have great respect for fish and the environment. They show this respect by using catch and release and honoring fishing **limits**.

Catch and Release

Unhooking a fish quickly is important for catch and release. A fish's gills take oxygen from water. A fish out of water can't breathe. Most anglers catch and release fish they don't plan to eat. This helps to **conserve** the fish population. Some anglers try to unhook the fish while it is in the water. If that is not possible, the next best option is to get the fish back in the water as soon as possible. Handle the fish with care, gripping it behind the gills. Don't squeeze too hard. If the fish is very tired, you may need to move it gently through the water to revive it.

A fish that comes to the boat bleeding, with damaged gills, or that is hooked badly should be kept rather than tossed back. It is unlikely to survive. If you are catching and keeping fish as part of your limit, try to return a healthy one to the water and keep the hurt one.

limit—the number of fish a person can legally catch and take home in a specific amount of time
conserve—to save

Remember that fishing only up to your limit is not just a good idea, it's also the law. Check with your state department of natural resources to find out how many fish you can legally keep. You may also need to buy a license, depending on your area. Your state department of natural resources may also have activities or fishing clubs for you to join.

Fishing and the Environment

When you are fishing, it's important to pay attention to how you affect the environment. Lead **sinkers** and fake baits containing lead are often small and easily misplaced. They also can be lost in the water when a line snaps. Loons, ducks, swans, and other water birds sometimes eat lost lead baits and sinkers. This gives them lead poisoning, which is deadly. Always try to be responsible with your baits and equipment.

sinker—a small weight that makes bait sink deeper into a body of water

Part of being a good angler is keeping the environment clean. Never leave any of your fishing gear behind. Littering with unwanted fishing gear such as bad line and broken lures can be even worse than littering with pop cans and candy wrappers. Animals can get tangled up in discarded line. Birds sometimes use the line when making their nests. Chicks can get caught in the line and die.

Most anglers really love nature. They work hard to protect the environment. They help make sure that other anglers will also be able to enjoy fishing for years to come.

FACT
Biodegradable line is new to the sport of fishing. Normally fishing line takes 600 years to break down. Biodegradable fishing line breaks down in just five years.

GLOSSARY

angler (ANG-glur)—a person who fishes

bait (BAYT)—something used to attract fish

barb (BARB)—a sharp piece of metal that extends from behind a fish hook's point

conserve (kuhn-SURV)—to save

leader (LEE-duhr)—a short piece of wire that connects a fishing line to the bait

limit (LIM-it)—the number of fish a person can legally catch and take home in a specific amount of time

lure (LOOR)—a fake bait used in fishing

sinker (SINGK-ur)—a small weight that makes bait sink deeper into a body of water

sonar (SOH-nar)—a device that uses sound waves to find underwater objects; sonar stands for sound navigation and ranging

spinnerbait (SPIN-ur-bayt)—a fake bait with blades that spin when it is pulled through the water

stringer (STRING-ur)—a string, wire, or chain with snaps that hold fish

READ MORE

Ross, Nick. *Fishing*. Get Outdoors. New York: PowerKids Press, 2010.

Schwartz, Tina P. *Freshwater Fishing*. Reel It In. New York: PowerKids Press, 2012.

Walker, Andrew. *How to Improve at Fishing*. How to Improve at—. New York: Crabtree Pub., 2009.

INTERNET SITES

FactHound offers a safe, fun way to find Internet sites related to this book. All of the sites on FactHound have been researched by our staff.

Here's all you do:

Visit *www.facthound.com*

Type in this code: 9781429684224

Super-cool stuff! Check out projects, games and lots more at
www.capstonekids.com

INDEX